Dedication

This book is dedicated to my three daughters, who gave
me emotional and spiritual support, and stuck with me,
through the most difficult and challenging times of my life.
Thank you Rachel, Jamie and Jenifer.

I love you.

Acknowledgements

I want to thank my sisters, brother and parents
for loving me and giving me some great stories to tell.

I would also like to thank my friend Jonni
and my editor, Jeanette Nofri, for helping me
get my forty plus years of memories down on paper
and in good enough shape for other people to read.

THIS IS NOT MY LIFE

Table of Contents

PART FOUR

PART FIVE

PART ONE

My First Childhood Memory

One of my earliest childhood memories is in 1969 when my family was living in Everett, Washington. I was five years old. My twin brother Mike and I were in the back yard of our house throwing rocks over the fence into our neighbor's garden. The neighbor came running out, yelling, "If you throw one more rock in my garden I'm going to kill you."

This gave me a great idea. I told Mike we should call the cops to teach him a lesson that he can't threaten us. We went in the house, picked up the phone and dialed "0." I told the operator I needed to talk to the police. She asked me what was wrong and I told her a man was going to kill me and my brother. She asked if my dad was there – I said, "No, he is at work." She asked if my mother was there – I said, "She's asleep and we can't wake her up." My mom worked the graveyard shift and gave us strict instructions not to wake her up. My grandfather was in the basement, but the operator didn't ask if my grandfather was there.

The police and fire department came out to our house because the operator thought my mom was dead and a man was trying to kill us. My mom and grandfather were very upset with us for calling the police. But the cops said it was good that we called because the guy did threaten to kill us. The cops

1

spoke to the neighbor and informed him that it was against the law to threaten children. Having a twin brother made it a lot easier to get into trouble, because he always agreed with everything I said.

I knew the neighbor wasn't really going to kill us, but I also knew he would get in trouble if I called for help. At that point, I realized I could talk my way out of anything.

My First Business Plan

Later that year we moved from Everett, Washington to Las Vegas. On the road trip down, my mother gave me and my brother a bag of marshmallows. I told Mike, "Don't eat them all. When we get to Vegas we're going to sell them." My brother asked how much we could get for a marshmallow. I told him, "At least a dollar for each marshmallow. They're really good. Everyone's going to want one. We can make a lot of money off these marshmallows."

We were so excited to arrive at our new home. We thought it would be a good idea to sell our marshmallows door to door to our new neighbors. We could meet them and also see if they had any kids. When the neighbors opened their doors, we asked, "Would you like to buy a marshmallow? They are a dollar each." We'd hold an individual marshmallow in our hands for them to inspect before purchasing. We sold marshmallows to nearly every home on the block. This was a great business plan.

At the fourth house, though, with my sales pitch ready and the marshmallow in my hand, the lady of the house said, "That marshmallow is dirty. No one will buy it for a dollar."

"They won't?" I asked.

"No," She said. I asked her how much a marshmallow was. "Nothing," she said, "You can't buy just one marshmallow." I was shocked to find out that a marshmallow wasn't worth anything, because people had just paid us a dollar for them.

I went home and told my dad. He laughed and explained that they were not really worth a dollar a piece, but that the neighbors bought the marshmallows because of my great sales pitch. "You can sell anything," he said.

He thought it was funny, but I was very serious about it. My first business plan had failed.

My First Flirtation

At the start of the baseball season my parents purchased season tickets for our family. We always sat in the same seats and saw the same people who sat near us. One person made a big impression on me. He always sat alone. Whenever I saw him I'd smile and wave, and he would smile and wave back. He was a "little person" and I had never seen one before; he was my size, but a grown man.

Towards the end of the season he introduced himself to my parents and said, "You have the sweetest child. She is the only one who smiles and waves at me. Most kids pretend not to see me or just stare." He asked if he could buy me a soda. My mom said he didn't have to do that, but he insisted. He brought me a drink. He was so nice. I will never forget him and that day.

That was the first time I remember my mom telling me I was a flirt.

My First Encounter with Rudeness

When Mike and I were six years old, my dad took my brother to the barber shop for a buzz cut. My brother did not want his head shaved because he was afraid the other kids would make fun of him. My dad said it's hot here in Las Vegas and a buzz cut will make you cooler. My brother didn't care, he didn't want his hair cut.

The first day after Mike's buzz cut, on the way to school a kid yelled, "Hey, baldy!" My brother yelled back, "Your butt is bald." I laughed so hard. That was the first day I realized my brother was funny.

Then the kid said, "You guys are fat!"

I didn't know what *fat* was. I said, "I don't even know what that means."

"People that are big are fat," he said.

I felt stupid that I did not know what fat meant. In my family, we did not point out each other's differences or judge other people. I thought everybody was the same. I liked everyone and couldn't understand why people were mean to each other.

My Next Business Plan

When I was eight, I came up with a new way to make money. One day, walking down the street, I saw two guys pushing a grocery cart full of cans.

I asked them, "What are you doing with all those cans?" They said they were going to sell them to make money. I asked where they got the cans. They said behind the bars. So, I went home with a great idea: sell used aluminum cans for cash.

At that time, only beer cans were aluminum, but we also collected returnable glass. My brother and I got some trash bags. I told Mike we had to get up early in the morning so we could beat those two men to the cans.

We got up at 5 a.m. every day and collected cans. We went to bed with our clothes and our shoes on. When the alarm went off we'd get up and run outside to start collecting. After school the first thing we did was collect more cans from behind the bars.

My two cousins and sister also got involved in this new family business. We synchronized our clocks to be exactly the same. We met at my house and went out to collect cans before the men with the grocery cart could get them. We didn't mind getting up early because we knew at the end of the week we'd have some cash.

We made friends with a guy who lived behind one of the bars in a little camper. I told him we needed a better way to collect cans, because while we were at school those two guys were out gathering the cans that we wanted. He said we should have the most innocent looking kid, which was me, ask the bartenders to save the cans for us.

I went into each bar and told the bartenders a sad story, then asked them to save their cans for us to pick them up after school. I negotiated with seven bartenders to save their cans for us.

Later, I hired a couple of neighborhood kids to help us on Saturdays so we could quit collecting at noon. Then our dad took us to the recycling center to sell them. Afterwards, he'd take us out for pizza or we'd go to Circus Circus to play games.

We made enough money off the cans to never have to ask our parents for money. My parents were thrilled that we were out doing something productive.

I really liked this job. I thought it was pretty cool that I created something to help myself. It was fun, challenging, and at the end of the week, we always had some cash. We did see some things children shouldn't see, like drunks coming out of bars barely able to walk. I didn't understand at the time that the alcohol made them like that.

PART TWO

Moving To Missouri

I lived a happy childhood in Las Vegas, hanging out with my friends and family. I was very close to my two younger cousins who lived with us, off and on, when I was growing up. When my parents purchased a motor home we thought we were the coolest kids on the block.

We were a close-knit family and took yearly trips across the country in the motor home. We visited many states west of the Mississippi and national parks like the Grand Canyon, Yellowstone and Mt. Rushmore. We only stayed at camp-grounds with swimming pools because we all loved to swim.

No matter where we were, we always attended church on Sunday. My grandfather was a prominent figure in the Reorganized Latter Day Saints (RLDS), before the church broke up.

I remember one Sunday going to a big church in Independence, Missouri. It was very different than the other churches we had been to. It was decorated with stones and very pretty. I was hoping we would be able to attend this church on a regular basis.

My mother said this place was the New Zion, and that all Christians would migrate to Missouri. Missouri was the Zion for the RLDS. I believed that living there would bring us to the next step in our lives.

My mother believed that Jesus would be returning to Zion. She felt that since the world was going to end, the only place we would be safe would be in Zion. I was thrilled we were moving to Missouri.

In 1975, when I was eleven, we packed up and moved from Las Vegas to a forty-acre farm in Chilhowee, Missouri. I did not realize what I was giving up and how hard our lives would become.

I had to give up can-collecting because there were no bars allowed in our county, but as my mother reminded me, we all had to sacrifice to be closer to Jesus and live in this place.

My dad got a job at the local grainery. One day while he was at the top of the silo he slipped and fell three stories and landed on his right side. His entire body was black from bruising and he couldn't move for weeks. He was in a lot of pain and they thought the cold winter would make it worse. So, my dad moved back to Nevada, where he stayed and worked with my grandfather.

To me, it felt like my dad walked out of my life. Losing him made some very difficult years ahead even harder to bare. He'd come out and stay with us for the summer months. Since phone calls were expensive, we hardly spoke to him the rest of the year. I went from talking to my father every day to barely talking to him at all.

My dad sent us money, but it was never enough. My mom's salary as a nurse was cut in half when we moved to Missouri. She had to work two full-time jobs. She was always tired and we hardly ever saw her.

When my oldest sister, LeeAnn, left for college right after we moved, our family shrank to just my twin brother Mike, me and our sister, Leslie, who was thirteen months older. We were pretty much always home alone; days would go by without us seeing an adult.

Our lives had changed drastically, and we had no parental supervision. My sister took on the role of mom, and tried to boss us around. However, my brother and I soon converted her to "our side" and the three of us did a lot of crazy things.

At the time it seemed to me that my mother didn't really care about us anymore. She probably was exhausted most of the time, and didn't have the energy to deal with us. When, on the rare occasion, we did see her, she would be reading. I remember saying to her, "Mom...Mom...Mom," over and over, without her ever answering. My brother, sister and I knew we had to depend on each other for our survival.

The first year on the farm, during a storm, our well was hit by lightning. For the next four years we had no running water. We had to haul water up from a spring on our property. We filled five gallon buckets, one cup at a time. We had to carry the water several hundred yards up to the house and to the farm animals. We had 500 chickens, one horse and seven pigs. This farm was far bigger then we were able to handle, especially with no experience. The three of us worked hard every day. It was a very miserable time. We did not like living in Missouri.

We had many bunny rabbits that we sold at the market for pretty good money. As fast as they reproduced, we had money to help pay the family expenses.

On top of all this, the people of the town did not like us and called us "outsiders." It wasn't all bad, though. I learned many things that became very helpful when I grew up. I learned how to plant and maintain a garden without running water, and how to preserve fruits and vegetables – which would help me survive later on in my life. Not having running water taught me how important and precious water is. Every time I take a shower, I'm so thankful for the water that flows out of the tap, already warm and running freely. And I learned how to fish, something I grew to enjoy as an adult.

When we found out we could enter stuff in the county fair and earn money, we entered as many things as we could. We went through the house finding stuff to enter; we baked things from my mom's cookbook and entered them. The more things we entered, the more money we had. We never needed to ask our parents for money.

Working so hard on the farm made me physically strong. We had to face many challenges. I could choose to embrace them or ignore them. I embraced all the challenges.

The winters were often very harsh, with snow drifts more than six feet high. We had no farm equipment, but had to clear several hundred yards of driveway with nothing more than shovels, so my mother could get to work.

We learned that when it snowed we did not have to haul water. Instead we could shovel the snow into big metal pots, put the pots on the stove and melt it – which was a lot easier than hauling water. The water for the animals would freeze every couple of hours, so we'd have to break the ice and refill the containers.

My Dad

One winter, my parents traded our horse, Buck, for a wood stove in order to keep warm. I loved that horse; I learned to ride him bareback. The prior summer, when I went to ride him, he got spooked. He reared up and fell on me.

I was unable to move. My father ran over to help me, but I told him to just let me lay there a while and I would be all right. Every part of my body hurt. It probably scared my parents pretty bad, but I knew I was O.K. I wondered if that incident had anything to do with Buck getting traded for the wood stove. I didn't blame him for what happened.

Given it to do over again, I would not change a thing. Those years on the farm taught me so many valuable lessons I could not have learned otherwise. I know my parents did their best and never meant to put us through those hard times.

My Best Friend Tammy

A year after we moved to Chilhowee, I met a new friend at church, Tammy. Her mom moved them to Missouri for the same reason as my mom, to be close to Zion. She was an outsider, too, and shunned as badly as we were. Tammy became my best friend and a huge part of my life. The things we did together made living in Missouri a lot better. She was not just my friend, but a friend of our family and became like one of our sisters.

One time when we were walking to my house Tammy took out a book of matches. She lit one match and threw it in a ditch. We looked back and saw the brush on fire. The fire looked huge to us. We were really scared. We ran all the way to my house and hid. The fire must have been small enough to burn itself out, because no one ever noticed it.

When I look back, I realize we weren't such bad children. We just wanted to have fun, like all kids do. It was a lot easier to do things we shouldn't have without parents around. Some of the ways we found to entertain ourselves were not very nice, but it's what we did.

Joyriding

My mom took the pickup truck to work and left her car at home with the keys in it. When she was at work, Tammy, my siblings and I often took her car joyriding.

One day we filled a couple of 5-gallon buckets with eggs and egged every building in the town. All four of us hung out of the car windows and plastered the town. Since we had five hundred chickens we had a lot of eggs.

We egged the buildings for several days in a row and finally had to stop so we wouldn't get caught. After that, the town of Chilhowee created a law that anyone caught with eggs would be fined $50 per egg.

Coach Bhagat

When I was 14 I joined the girls' basketball team at
school. My coach, Mr. Bhagat, who was also the school
superintendent, was one of my few friends in Chilhowee.
We'd go to lunch and hang out.

I could do no wrong in this man's eyes. He let me get away
with a lot, even ditch school sometimes. He thought I was
smart, and encouraged me to develop my potential.

I set him up on a date with my sister, LeeAnn, but she said all
he did was talk about me. I guess I was a charming fourteen
year old.

I went to all the basketball games, but basically never
attended the 8th grade. He knew I hated the way the students
treated me, but told me I should attend my classes anyway.

I could not have imagined that my life was about to change
forever – and that I would no longer be able to be a teenager.
However, I believe that for every loss there is a gain, and I
gained much more then I lost.

My First Driving Lesson

I didn't know it at the time, but this would be my last year of
school in the town of Chilhowee, Missouri, population 302.
On the last day of school, a man in a military uniform, named

David, came up to me and my friend Tammy and asked us if we'd like to go for a ride in his car. An older guy wanting us to hang out and ride in his car was really cool. We got into his car and drove off.

He drove onto a dirt road and asked me if I knew how to drive. I said, "Yes, I drive all the time." He told us he had just bought the car – a mint condition Chevy Impala muscle car – with the money he got from his National Guard training.

He said I could drive his car if I wanted to. I got into the driver's seat. When we had gone a very short distance and I was about to turn a corner on the gravel road, he said, "Step on the gas pedal as hard as you can." That sounded like fun, so I did. As I took the corner, I hit five fence posts and totaled his car.

I had never driven a car before, so I didn't have the reflex to apply the brakes. We bounced all around the car because we were not wearing seat belts.

David jumped out and ran around the car, checking out the damage and yelling, "My car! My car!" His Impala was no longer in mint condition. The roof, the hood, and every door was dented.

I said, "I'm sorry. But, I'm fourteen years old, what do you expect?" Whenever my siblings and I took my mom's car out joyriding, my sister Leslie always drove. I was just thankful that none of us got hurt.

Someone was coming. David told us not to say anything; he would do the talking. He told the property owner that a dog jumped out in front of us, and when he swerved to miss the dog he took out the fence. He made arrangements with the farmer to replace the fence. He never mentioned the condition of his car again.

When he had to go on his two-week training, he asked to leave his car in our yard. While he was gone, I decided to make up for what I had done to his car by covering up the scratches with paint. I took 2 gallons of red barn paint and painted his car. I didn't know that it was oil-based paint that took a lot of time to dry. There were a lot of bugs in Missouri, and the car became a huge bug strip. The bugs landed all over his car and could not fly away. Boy, I thought, will he be surprised when he gets back.

When he saw his car he was speechless. It was old barn paint and I don't believe it ever dried. This is what happens when you let a fourteen year old drive your car and then let her babysit your car. David later donated the car to the Chilhowee School for a fundraiser. Apparently, he had a bad reputation in the town. People lined up to pay $1 for 3 hits on the car with a sledge hammer.

PART THREE

A Loss of Innocence

David and I became friends. He hung out at my house the whole summer and we had a good time together. One day he said he had a surprise for me and wanted me to meet him outside later that night.

He had a blanket on the ground next to our old barn. We sat and talked and then started making out. I told him to stop, but he continued. Though I struggled against his 200 lb. frame with all my strength, he was able to pull off my pants.

As I fought against him, he kept saying he loved me and everything would be fine. I had no control over this situation. The harder I fought, the harder he fought me. I was so scared and didn't know what to do. I was very naive about sex. I couldn't put a name to what he was doing, but I knew it was wrong. I wanted to run away as fast as I could and never come back. But I couldn't get away. He held me down and raped me.

Afterwards, I just laid there and didn't say anything. I guess I was in shock. He put his arm around me and said he loved me and that he was sorry. Somehow, I thought it was my fault. I felt horrible. I didn't say a word. I just walked away.

I went back to the house and up to my room and shut the door. The next day I was sore and bruised, sad and confused. I didn't tell anyone about it because I thought the whole thing was my fault and felt embarrassed and ashamed.

I didn't tell anyone what happened that night. It's a very hard thing to tell someone when you're just 14 years old. I kept the pain inside for a long time. I didn't want to upset my parents, and I didn't want anyone to feel sad for me either. I decided I needed to wise up and take control of my own life; I did not need anyone else to take care of me.

A couple of days later, David knocked on the door wanting to talk to me. He assured me that everything was O.K. and that he still loved me. I thought no one else would ever want me now. He promised to marry and take care of me for the rest of my life. After all, he said, his mother married when she was fifteen. He said when I turned fifteen we'd get married.

Soon after that, when he got his check from the military, he convinced me to run away with him and get married in another state. I thought, 'O.K., I'll marry him and we'll live happily ever after.'

He took me across several state lines. My mother was very upset when she found out. We drove to Omaha, Nebraska, where he said we were going to start a new life. But, we ended up sleeping in his car and had no food. So, we headed to Kansas where his parents lived.

As soon as we got there, David's parents said my mom called and was very worried about me; I was to come home right away. I think part of the reason I ran off with him was that I wanted to start a new life away from Missouri.

I returned home and told my mother I had decided to marry this man. She wanted to have him prosecuted for statutory rape since he took me across state lines. I begged her not to press charges and she finally gave in. I think my mother was worried I'd run away again, but I never would have. Running away with him was very scary. He did a poor job of taking care of me.

We got married three days after I turned fifteen.

Truly Hungry

We moved into a small house in Chilhowee, Missouri, that belonged to David's grandmother. I got pregnant right away. He had no job and we had no money. My friend Tammy stopped by on her way to school to ask if I would come to her house for dinner that night; they were having spaghetti. I had not eaten in two weeks. I was so hungry, I said yes. I was several months pregnant and weighed less than 100 lbs.

But, David refused to let me go. He said we could eat at our own home. We had five pounds of flour and salt. I made noodles, boiled them, and that is what we ate until the flour ran out. I truly know what it is to be hungry.

I didn't want to admit to my parents that it was a mistake to marry David. Besides, since I made the decision to marry him, I thought I just had to live with it. I was unaware that things like charities or social services even existed. When my mother found out I was pregnant, she insisted we move in with her. She made sure I had healthy food and vitamins.

David Finally Gets a Job

A few months later, while I was still pregnant, David got a good job with the railroad and we moved back into his grandmother's house.

I was so excited, thinking that he would be able to provide for us and everything would be fine. We could live happily ever after in that little house. I had always wanted a normal life with a normal family.

One day he came home and said he got fired. Knowing that he lied about most things, I didn't believe him and called his boss. His boss told me that David had quit. I couldn't believe he would throw away a good job with a new wife and a baby due in a few weeks. I begged his boss to take him back, which he agreed to do. Then I had to plead with David to go back, for the baby's sake. He did go back for about a month, then he quit again.

Rachel

Rachel was born in July of 1980. It was a very difficult delivery. I was in hard labor for four days. My doctor was gone on vacation and the other doctor was afraid to do a C-section on a 15-year-old girl.

While Rachel was in the birth canal my blood pressure went really high. My mom told our friends and family in the waiting room that I might not make it. I had no idea until a week or two later that I was so close to death.

We stayed in his grandmother's house for a while, but we ended up homeless and without food again. But, this time I had a daughter to feed, and was willing to ask for help. I got food stamps and other benefits that helped us get along.

Tammy is Betrayed

When Rachel was five months old, my friend Tammy invited me and Rachel to spend the night at her house. Tammy and I stayed up late talking. During our conversation Tammy broke down and told me that while I was in the hospital having Rachel, David locked her in our house and raped her.

I cried for three days. I felt so sad and guilty and horrible for the pain David caused her. I couldn't bring myself to tell her that he had done the same thing to me, because I felt so guilty. She was only 15 years old. I hated him for what he did to my friend.

I wanted to leave him but I was afraid. I had no education and had never had a job. I didn't think Rachel and I could survive on our own.

We Move to Washington

In April of 1981 we took our income tax refund check and moved to Tacoma, Washington. My sister LeeAnn, who lived in Tacoma, said it would be easier for David to find a job there. I liked it because Rachel and I could ride the bus for 50 cents. We rode the bus everywhere.

David got a job at a gas station. My days were free, so I could do anything I wanted. My sister lived in an adjoining apartment. One day she told me that some of their property was stolen and pawned under my name. I asked David about it and, of course, he denied it. He probably did steal and pawn my sister's stuff. He lied about most everything.

Rachel and I had a good time in Tacoma, but I wasn't about to forget what David had done to me and to Tammy.

We Weren't Important

A month later, David quit his job. I was now pregnant with
my second child. Our only option seemed to be to move back
to Missouri and stay at my mother's. David dropped us at my
mom's house and then drove off without saying where he was
going. A few days later, a friend knocked on the door and
told me that David had been arrested for breaking into a gas
station and stealing tootsie rolls and cigarettes.

I was embarrassed and humiliated. I didn't understand why
he would steal things instead of just getting a job. He was a
liar, a cheat and a rapist. I couldn't believe I was married to
such a loser. All I wanted to do was leave him.

My mother told me that if I left him she would help me.
Right after we heard that David was out of jail, my mom had
to go out of town for two weeks. She was afraid he'd come
after me and didn't want me staying at the house alone. So, I
went to stay with Tammy.

While I was there, I met a friend of hers, a really nice guy
named Curtis. One day he asked what I was going to name
the baby. I told him if it was a boy, I would name it Curtis
because I really liked his name.

Even though my mother hadn't returned yet, I was anxious to go back to her house. I didn't think David would still be looking there for me, since I hadn't been at the house for nearly two weeks. Within an hour of going back, David showed up. I told him I was leaving him and never wanted to see him again.

He said I was not leaving with his daughter and tried to take Rachel away from me. There was no way I was going to let him walk off with my daughter. I had to promise I wouldn't break up with him, to keep him from taking Rachel. I knew my parents would be home soon; I could put up with David for another two days. It was two days of pure hell. He wouldn't let me go anywhere, do anything or talk to anyone. I was afraid, but all I could do was pretend I was going to stay with him.

When my parents drove up, I went outside with Rachel in my arms. David came outside just as my mother was opening the car door. He had no idea what I was going to say. I told her that David wouldn't leave and was trying to take Rachel away from me. It didn't take my mother long to get rid of him. She threatened to call the police and he left.

My parents informed me that they were moving to Las Vegas and I was welcome to go with them. My mom was an ICU nurse, and wanted to move to Vegas because an RN made $20 an hour there. As an RN in Missouri, she made $6 an hour.

We loaded up the car and the truck and moved to Las Vegas.

Baby Curtis

Within a few months of moving to Las Vegas, my father retired and my mother got a job at the University Medical Center. She took me to all my doctor appointments while I was pregnant. My parents started buying things for the baby, but I asked them to stop because I had a feeling that the baby would be delivered dead.

In January of 1982, when I was 17, I had a baby boy. Everyone said my baby was healthy. The doctor said he was crying when he was born, but I did not hear him cry. I was convinced he was going to be born dead, but here he was alive and healthy at 6 lbs. 6 oz. I named him Curtis.

When the nurses brought the baby to me for his feedings, I told them something was wrong with the baby. He seemed too tired to eat, so I just cuddled with him.

The next day they did not bring Curtis to me. My brother called and I told him to send mom to take me home because the baby was going to die. When my mom arrived she talked to the nurse while I got dressed.

The baby had a problem with his heart. They wanted to transfer him to another hospital. They reassured me he would be O.K. I told the nurse my baby was going to die and I was leaving.

She asked me to sign some papers, but I refused. I just couldn't deal with it at the time.

As I was leaving the hospital I saw my dad. He asked me what was wrong. I said, "The baby is dying." I didn't show any emotion, I didn't want him to feel bad. I was sad, but held back my tears so my family wouldn't see it. I thought I had to be strong. On the drive home my mother tried to reassure me everything would be fine. I'm sure she knew I was hurting and was trying to be strong for them.

When we got home I got Rachel and lay down on my bed. My mom came in and told me that I needed to sign papers at the hospital where Curtis was taken.

At the hospital, the doctor said that I had to see the baby before he would tell me what was wrong with him. I told him I could not look at him again, but the doctor insisted. When we walked into the neonatal intensive care unit the baby was gasping for air. His little chest was sunken in. He didn't look anything like he did the last time I saw him. I think the doctor forced me to look at him because I was seventeen and he didn't think I would make the right decision. But, it was wrong to make me see him suffering. The doctor said that they could do a heart transplant and keep him alive as long as possible. Or we could just let him go. I told him to double the pain medication and let him go. I had to fight back my tears the whole time. All I wanted to do was get out of there as fast as I could and forget what I just saw. The doctor looked shocked at what I said. I told him the decision was not mine to make, that it had already been made.

A couple of days later we got the call that he had passed away. It was a relief that the ordeal was finally over. I learned that people and our children are not our possessions. They come into our lives for us to love and take care of. They can be taken from us at any time and we need to be able to let go. I will always remember my baby Curtis.

Night School

My mom thought I needed to get out of the house. She suggested that my brother and I go to night school. To me, night school was a place to mess around while my mom watched Rachel.

I made a new friend, Robin. She and I would eat sunflower seeds and put the shells under my brother Mike's desk, which really made him mad – I laughed for the first time since Curtis died. Mike was, and still is, my best friend. He stood by me through hard times and we always had fun together.

We attended night school for a month before we all dropped out. We had a really good time fooling around and getting away from life. I spent the summer at the swimming pool with Rachel and dated a little bit.

We moved to a house across town when Rachel was three. I got a job working at the Showboat Hotel and Casino's bowling alley as an official scorekeeper. It was a pretty fun job. My mother watched Rachel while I worked, and she went to work at night when I got home.

Ken

During the two years I worked at the Showboat, I dated a man named Ken and it became serious. He was a big, handsome man who was kind, gentle and caring. I adored him and wanted to spend the rest of my life with him. He made me feel special and important.

Every Sunday we got together for breakfast and hung out with Rachel at the park. Every Friday night was our date night. He would pay my brother Mike to babysit Rachel. We usually didn't hang out on Saturdays because I had no babysitter. We planned to get married in a year or so, after my divorce from David was final.

One Sunday Ken didn't show up. I was hurt, and didn't understand why he didn't call. I thought maybe he was mad at me. Later that day, my mother got a call from his mom saying that she had found him dead in bed. She didn't know how to tell me, so she asked that my mom explain what happened, and that she was very sorry.

My friends told me that he overdosed on Quaaludes and alcohol. I knew he drank, but I wasn't aware of any drug use. I never drank and didn't do drugs and didn't understand why people did. I was devastated and heartbroken. I had just turned 19. I had to remind myself that I did not "own" Ken. I enjoyed him for a short time in my life, and now it was time to let him go. I will always love and remember Ken.

PART FOUR

Sid

The loss of Ken was devastating. I just wanted to start my life over again. I wanted a stable life for me and Rachel. I wanted to be married and have a family life.

I started dating a man named Sid. He was nine years older than me, bald and not very attractive. I wasn't in love with him. I liked the fact that his family was religious. I assumed he was, too, which was important to me at the time.

Within days of starting to date he asked me to marry him. He told me he would help pay for my divorce from David, and we could get married as soon as it was final. Within weeks I was divorced. It doesn't take long to get a divorce in Las Vegas.

Sid and I were married in December of 1983, less than two months after meeting. It was too soon, but I was desperate for security. I certainly didn't know him very well. My daughter needed a father and deserved a better life than I was giving her. I didn't think I could make it on my own. I felt like I needed a man in my life.

One of the first things I wanted to do after we got married was buy a house. After my experience with David, I was determined to never be homeless again. At the age of 19, I bought my first home in Las Vegas.

31

Sid let me know before we got married that he did not drink or do drugs. This was a very important thing for me, as I wanted to bring my daughter up in a normal, happy family.

Six days after we were married, Sid came home from work carried by his friends. He had fallen off a forklift. He said he slipped on a piece of roofing material that had fallen on the forklift and fell two stories. He broke his pelvis and couldn't work for six weeks. While he was recuperating, his friends told me what really happened. He had been drinking on the job and that's why he fell off the forklift.

I felt betrayed by his lying about drinking and wanted to leave him. But, I couldn't bring myself to admit that I had made another terrible mistake. I didn't want to tell my parents; I was afraid they'd say 'I told you so.' I found out later that he not only drank alcohol, but smoked pot, too. I would never have married him if he had been honest with me, which he knew.

We had our first daughter, Jamie, one year later, in December, 1984. Our second daughter, Jenifer, was born in October, 1987. Sid was unable to work because of pain in his back and legs, which he blamed on the forklift accident.

First Abuse By Sid

About six months after Jenifer was born Sid helped my sister Leslie with some maintenance on her home. When I picked him up, Leslie told me that he drank a whole bottle of tequila and he was abusive towards her.

Driving home in the car he started yelling. I knew he was drunk, but I had no idea why he was angry. I didn't know that some people got angry after drinking alcohol.

When we got home I took Jenifer into the house. Sid went into the bedroom and got his gun. He pointed it at me and said, "You have five seconds to leave."

I took the baby and left as fast as I could. I shut the car door and heard a gun shot. As I sped off I heard four more shots. My heart was racing. Thank goodness my other two kids were staying at their Grandparents' house for the Easter weekend. I spent the night at Leslie's.

When I got home the next day, there were five gun shot holes in my bedroom window. Sid said he was not shooting at me, he just wanted to scare me. It worked. I remember wondering what on earth I had done to make him so angry. After that, Sid decided we should move to Utah to be closer to his family. I didn't want to move, but Sid was very insistent. Being a "good wife," I agreed to go.

We Move to Utah

In September, 1991, we moved to Kanab, Utah, a small town in the middle of nowhere. We paid off and rented out our house in Las Vegas and bought another house in Utah. I knew that buying houses was a good investment, but being a property owner made me feel even more trapped in my situation – my sense of responsibility to my tenants became another "reason" to put off leaving Sid.

Once he got us out of the state of Nevada, he didn't want me to talk to my family anymore. He started secretly recording my phone conversations. Anytime I went somewhere, including to the store, he accused me of sleeping around. I had no freedom at all after we moved to Utah.

He became increasingly violent. He threatened me almost every day. He started drinking a lot. The more he drank, the more violent he was and the scarier life became. The kids and I were afraid of him. He warned me that if I ever left him, he'd hunt me down and kill me and my whole family. He said, "You'll never get out of this alive."

One day a friend of Sid's gave him four Xanax pills to get high. Side effects include mental or mood problems, making my situation extremely dangerous. He downed the pills with a beer. Then we went to a parade in town. I was worried and stressed the entire time, but the kids had a good time.

Driving home, he started going faster and faster. The kids were in the back seat and I was terrified. I put my foot on the brake and stopped the car. Then I put the gear in "park" and took the keys out of the ignition. He punched me in the face with his fist. He grabbed the keys back and continued driving home. Someone in another car witnessed what happened and reported it to the police. The cops arrived at our house 10 minutes later.

As Officer Cram approached the door, Sid picked up his gun. He knocked on the door and Sid pointed the gun through the curtain at him. Sid told me that if I didn't get rid of him, the officer would be the first one dead, then me, then the kids and himself. I had no doubt he was fully capable of following through with his threats, because he followed through with them in the past. I opened the door. Officer Cram said he had a report that my husband had hit me. I told him that was not true. He asked me if I was O.K. I said, yes. He asked if my children were O.K. I said, yes, will you please go. Then he left.

After the Officer left, Sid argued a bit. I took the children in the other room, locked the door and put on a movie. Sid passed out. The whole night I thought about escaping – but felt I had no where to go. I had no money, no education and no job.

My three daughters, Rachel, Jamie, Jenifer and I talked about how we'd escape. But, because of his threats to my family, I knew that once we left we'd never be able to contact my parents or siblings again; we'd be in hiding. I believed that wherever we went he'd find us and kill us.

I was unable to protect myself or my children from this monster. I felt alone, with no one to turn to. I hated to admit to others, and to myself, how bad things really were.

I Get a Job

Part of the reason I was hesitant to leave Sid was that my education only went through the 8th grade and I didn't think I could get a job. I decided to get some kind of training. My mother suggested I become a certified nursing assistant, which I did. This made it possible for me to get a job at Kane County Hospital. I felt a little bit freer and that much closer to escaping Sid's abuse. Having a job gave me a sense of independence that helped me believe I could take care of my kids when we left.

At the time, I thought I wasn't smart enough to get a good-paying job. That's why I wanted to buy houses, it was a way I could feel successful in life. At the age of 24, I owned two homes. By the time I was 30, I had paid off two of several homes I owned by then.

Sid Threatens Our Family

One day when my daughters and I arrived home from the local swimming pool and saw that Sid had been drinking. He pointed a gun at us and said, "You have five seconds to leave." We ran to the van as fast as we could. As I pulled away he broke the window of the front door of the house and yelled, "Don't go to your mother's or I'll go there and kill you all."

I didn't have any cash on me, but I had a Discover card in my pocket and no ID. I had no shoes on and my kids had no shoes. I filled up the gas tank of the van and then we pulled over at a rest stop. It got pretty cold that night in the desert. We slept in the van. The whole time I was afraid he would find us. We talked about how our life was an adventure, and this was just one more adventure.

The next morning I drove to Las Vegas because it was familiar. I had no intention of seeing my parents, after his threats. I went to a K-Mart. I left the children in the van and went in, hoping people wouldn't notice that I was not wearing shoes. I got some snacks for the kids.

Next, I went to the Circus, Circus RV Park hoping they would take the Discover card, which they did. We spent three nights and four days there. The children and I acted like we had a normal life. It was just the four of us together and it was nice.

But, I decided to return home to Utah because I had a job and a house to take care of, and felt responsible to my tenants. I was too afraid to do anything else. I felt I wasn't in a position to do what I wanted to do – keep driving.

Working Double Shifts

My friend Vicky and I decided to get jobs at the nursing home in Hurricane, Utah. They would allow us to work 16 hour shifts. We both worked 16 hours on Saturday and Sunday. We'd go in at 7 a.m. on Saturday, and get off at 11 p.m. We'd sleep in the car and go back to work at 7 a.m. on Sunday and work until 11 p.m. We didn't get much rest. This type of schedule was considered a full-time job. We received decent benefits, and it allowed us more time to spend with our families. I had a great time working there and I loved my job.

Vicky and I became very close friends. Hurricane was about an hour's drive from where we lived. Vicky was having a hard time at home, too. We'd talk about how we were going to escape our lives, pack up our kids, drive away and never go back.

My Parents Get Sick

In May of 1995 my mother got really sick. I constantly worried about how sick she was, and my dad wasn't much better. It made it nearly impossible for me to work. When both my parents were put in intensive care at the same time, I took time off to be with them.

My mother had never been sick before, so I knew whatever was wrong was not good. She was later diagnosed with cancer. Two weeks later she was still in the hospital. I went to see her on her birthday, July 9, 1995. I was shocked when I opened the door and saw that she was dying. I walked over to her bed and she gave me a big hug and told me that she loved me. We did not talk much after that. She died two hours later. She was 58.

Later that summer I took the kids with me to live at my dad's house in Las Vegas because Sid had given Rachel a black eye. She was trying to stop him from hitting me.

My dad's house was too small for all of us because my sister Leslie and my brother Mike were living with him at the time. So, we moved into my dad's motor home which was parked outside his house. It wouldn't start but we didn't care. I got a job with a temporary agency as a certified nursing assistant, and enrolled the kids in school.

One day Sid showed up and offered to fix the motor home. While he was working on it, the carburetor caught fire. The fire destroyed the entire motor home. Now we had nowhere to live. We had no choice but to go home.

When we got back to Utah, I wanted to get Rachel out of the situation with Sid as soon as possible. The only thing I could think of was the Job Corps. This was the hardest thing I had ever done in my life. I felt I was abandoning her, but I knew I had to set her free. It was the only way she'd be safe from Sid.

Fortunately, she grew to love Job Corps and did really well; she even excelled. I was so thankful and happy for her.

My father's health got worse. I drove the 200 miles to Las Vegas twice a month to help take care of him. His doctor told me he had cancer and she wanted to start his treatment the next day. But my dad asked me to take him back home and just let him go. I took care of him until he died two weeks later, July 19, 1996 – one year and ten days after my mother passed away.

I Take a Much-Needed Break

In February of 1997, my friend Vicky and I decided to go on a cruise. My parents had passed away within a year of each other and I had taken over the responsibility of trying to help two of my siblings who had drug problems. I was very stressed out. Even Sid could see that I needed a break and agreed that the trip was a good idea.

Vicky drove us from Kanab, Utah to Long Beach, California, where the ship was docked. We went from Long Beach to Catalina Island and then to Ensenada, Mexico. We had a really good time on Catalina Island. I called home to check on the kids and make sure that Sid was there. I did not trust him. Everything seemed fine at home.

We had a really nice dinner on the ship and began planning our next day in Ensenada. The next morning, I told Vicky I had an awful feeling that Sid was in Ensenada and I did not want to leave the ship. She tried to convince me that Sid was still in Utah. When we got off the ship, there he was, waiting at the terminal.

He had driven all the way from Utah to Ensenada, just to be there when we got off the ship. He said, "I wanted to surprise you." I think he expected to catch me with another man. I was livid; really pissed off and he knew it. I refused to go anywhere with him. Vicky and I went our separate ways for the day. I assume Sid turned around and drove back to Utah.

I knew I could not live like this much longer. I could not continue putting my kids through this kind of life. I had to find a way out, even if it meant us being on the run for the rest of our lives.

When I got home, I began selling some houses and paying off our debt. I was close to leaving Sid and wanted to pay off my debts before I did.

Church

Before my mother passed away, I made a deal with my father-in-law that if I went to church faithfully, our lives would be a lot better. I tried telling my in-laws how bad things were, but their answer was always, go to church. All my problems would be solved if I prayed about them and went to church.

I had been attending this LDS church for six Sundays and no one came up to me or my children to welcome us. It was a very small town and everyone knew my husband was disabled and unable to help me. Yet, not one person from the church stopped by or called to see how we were doing.

During a testimony Sunday, I stood up and told them I had a problem with the lack of fellowship at the church. I told them my decision to attend the LDS church was not easy because I was raised in the RLDS church, which believes their church is wrong. One lady came up to me afterwards and said, "I didn't know you were a member of this church; that's why I never talked to you."

Later that day, I received a phone call from the Bishop's secretary saying he wanted to see me. I asked the missionary president, Brother Beard, to attend the meeting with me. The Bishop heard about what I said in church and was angry. He told me never to return to his church. Brother Beard said to me, "If I hadn't been there, I would not have believed you." I never went back to that church.

I Access the Internet and Leave Sid

On December 4, 1997 we got a Web-TV installed and I was able to access the internet. This was huge. I suddenly had a connection with other people and the outside world.

I met people online who gave me the courage to leave my husband. I was online all the time. I was able to talk to people about my situation in a safe environment. It was like finding freedom. I finally had a connection outside of my abusive world.

During the next two months, I was able to find the courage to leave Sid. On February 16, 1998 I left him. With both my parents gone, I no longer had to fear that Sid would kill them.

I moved to Saint George, Utah with my two youngest daughters. Rachel was still in the Job Corps. We lived in a tiny trailer with no running water, but we adapted well. I bought a gym membership and the kids got in free after 5 p.m. That's where my kids took their showers and swam in the pool. I always told them life is an adventure and we had to make it as much fun as we could.

I got a job in Cedar City, Utah at a Rehab Center. I worked weekends; 16 hour shifts on Saturday and Sunday, with eight hours off between shifts. I slept in my car because the commute was over an hour each way. Leaving my kids home alone was very difficult for me but they knew the drill. When answering the phone, mom was asleep or in the shower.

Jamie and Jenifer could both cook, so they took care of themselves on weekends. Sometimes they spent the weekend with their father or his parents in Saint George.

One of the men who worked at the Rehab Center asked me to go to the movies with him. I said, yes, and picked, "As Good As It Gets" starring Jack Nicholson. I started laughing during the movie and realized that this was the first time I had laughed in a very long time. I could not even remember the last time I enjoyed a movie. I was always afraid and stressed when I was with Sid. It surprised me that I was able to feel relaxed and actually have some fun.

Leaving Sid

I looked forward to starting a new life that did not include Sid. I was anxious to leave my life of constant fear of both Sid and not being able to take care of my kids on my own.

I moved from Kanab to Saint George, Utah, 80 miles from Sid. I had to stay in Utah because I was only certified to work in Utah. I constantly worried that Sid would be outside my door. When I had to leave the trailer at night, I'd call the house in Kanab to make sure Sid was there, so I wouldn't have to worry that night.

I had few possessions because if Sid threatened us, I knew I'd have no time to pack. Sid said if I left him I'd be looking over my shoulder for the rest of my life – so far he was right.

Now I realize that this period of my life created my "fight or flight" syndrome, also known as a sympathetic response, a natural reaction to trauma. It is common in people who suffer PTSD (Post Traumatic Stress Disorder).

I was lonely and needed emotional support to continue my life away from Sid.

Internet Boyfriend, Tim

While still living in Saint George, Utah, I started an online relationship with a man named Tim in Dayton Ohio. His friendship gave me the courage to keep moving forward. I could tell him anything without him judging me. On days I wasn't sure I could keep going, he'd be there with encouragement.

I never met Tim in person, yet to this day I maintain a close friendship with him. Tim was my only friend for a long time. He was sweet and kind and the only person I trusted.

Since we talked every day, our phone bills got expensive, which neither of us could afford. I was so in need of company, I began chatting online with people who lived closer.

My relationship with Tim changed when I heard him light a cigarette. and then the sound of him smoking pot. I thought, 'Oh my gosh!' I could never be with someone who smoked pot or cigarettes. I realized I had made up a fantasy about him, and didn't really know the man. I guess I created the fantasy because he supported and encouraged me.

Sylvia

I met Sylvia when I was working at a nursing home in Hurricane, Utah. She had MS and most people did not like her because she was so ornery.

When new people came to work at the facility, their initiation was to work with her. One time a new employee who was working with her went to lunch and never came back. But, I found Sylvia very intriguing. It didn't take me long to form a friendship with her; I was willing to be friends with anyone.

Sylvia was so mean she got just about anything she wanted. She had a cat from hell that lived with her. Everybody feared it because it acted like her and was mean to everyone. Sylvia was the only one in the nursing home with her room painted a color other than white.

As I got to know Sylvia I discovered that she was a really fun, nice person. The more time I spent with her, the nicer she became to everyone else. She had lived a very active lifestyle before contracting MS and as it progressed she became harder to deal with. I realized that she just needed someone who cared.

Sylvia and I decided to call the desk at the nursing home and say I need to talk to my brother Mike. The gal at the desk asked for his last name, so I said it was Hunt. We listened to her page on the loud speaker, Mike Hunt....Mike Hunt, over and over. Sylvia and I laughed so hard – we were easily entertained.

One day the nursing home gave Sylvia a thirty day notice because she had tape recorded a nurse refusing to give her water. Evidence, she told them, she was going to use against them. I got her a lawyer and he informed the nursing home that they could not kick her out. Then I got her a web-TV so she could complain to everyone online about the nursing home. Little did I realize this would open a new door for her -- a way to escape her reality.

Sylvia used my picture, instead of her own, to collect online boyfriends. She made up stories about herself until the men would catch her in lies because she'd forget what she said previously. She kept track of the men in a journal. She laughed at the thought of one of these guys tracking her down and getting the surprise of their life – she was a three hundred pound woman with MS living in a nursing home.

Sylvia and I remained friends after I no longer worked at the nursing home. She was another person I could count on for encouragement to stay away from Sid.

PART FIVE

Intro Chuck

In July 1998 I answered a personal ad online by a man named Chuck who was looking for friendship. I couldn't commit to a relationship because I had to be ready to run at any time. I needed the freedom I had now. My first priority was keeping my kids and me safe.

Chuck and I exchanged emails. He was thirty-one years old and I was thirty-three. He described himself as six foot two, two hundred twenty-five pounds, with dark hair and blue eyes. He liked riding motorcycles, camping and hiking. I was amazed he was single.

He had been an F16 crew chief, responsible for the maintenance and mechanical work on one jet. He was working on getting a private pilot license, hoping to get a job with an airline. Wow! How honorable and proud he came across. I thought this guy was something special.

He said he was retired from the military with full benefits. I wondered how someone could retire with full benefits at his age. He told me his unit had been deployed in the Desert Storm war. I was impressed that he fought for our country and stood up for his beliefs.

Our emails were short, but we decided to exchange phone numbers. I couldn't wait to meet this guy who seemed like the perfect man. We had the same morals and standards and he didn't smoke, drink, or do drugs.

Meeting Chuck for the First Time

Chuck wanted to meet me on July 9, but my daughter Rachel was graduating from Job Corps that day and I would be going to Salt Lake City for the graduation. We made plans to meet the next day to go hiking in Zion National Park.

On the morning of July 10 Chuck called and asked me where I lived. I asked him why he was asking; he said because there was a plane flying over his house that he could also hear the plane over the phone. He had recently moved into a house just two blocks from where I lived. In fact, I walked by his house every day to drop my daughter off at school.

I was living in an RV park and I told him I would meet him on the playground. Jamie and Jenifer came with me. When he stepped out of his car I was impressed that he was very handsome, well dressed, clean cut and had a mustache. Getting to know his personality before we met made him even more attractive to me.

Jamie and Jenifer took down his license plate number and description of him and his car, just in case their mother didn't return. After years of abuse my kids obviously had trust issues and wanted to protect me.

After we drove off I asked to stop at the post office. It turned out that my mail box was only one down and one over from his. Another weird coincidence. I began to feel that the universe was pulling us together and maybe my parents in heaven were looking out for me.

We sat on a boulder in Zion National Park and talked for six hours. He was a good listener and very patient. We talked about our lives growing up and he said he had five younger sisters and was the only boy. He was raised in a strict LDS family in Southern California. He talked about his dream of building a business, but that he had been married to someone who held him back and didn't let him grow as a person.

He said the next time he got married he would marry his best friend. I knew that I would be his best friend and we would be married and live a life that I had only dreamed about.

He had a list of things he wanted in a wife. He said he wanted to marry someone who was a twin. This shocked me because I was a twin, and hadn't mentioned it yet. He said he felt that twins have a special bond that single birth people don't have. When I told him I had a twin brother, he was surprised. We both thought it was a weird coincidence. As we talked I felt we were meant to be together.

He told me he retired from the military at the age of 22. I asked how he could retire at such a young age. He explained that running after jets in those big boots blew out his knees. He could no longer do his job, so the military offered him full medical and disability. He said the offer was the same as a retired full bird colonel retiring after thirty years. He could not turn the offer down, he said, so he retired.

The fact that he had not worked since then raised questions in my mind. He was able to convince me that all of this was a reasonable explanation that I could accept. He always had a good explanation.

He said he was going to a motorcycle rally later that month, and asked if I wanted to go with him, but I had to work.

I told him I was recently separated and filing for divorce from my husband of fourteen years. I did not go into detail regarding my relationship with Sid because I wasn't ready to share that part of my life.

I told him I was a certified nursing assistant and worked at local nursing homes, and that I had some rental properties; the houses I still owned and my car were all paid for.

When I told him I had been married since I was fifteen years old, he was surprised. I did not go into details about any of my relationships.

During our conversation I mentioned that when I was sixteen my two cousins and I dressed up my two-year-old nephew in my daughter Rachel's clothes and took him to Sears for pictures. We named him Alexis. My mom and sister were very upset that we took pictures of him dressed as a girl. My mom would not let us buy the pictures, though I fully intended to buy them. Chuck laughed and said it was a cute story. We had a really good time.

The Day After

The next day Chuck called and said, let's go hiking at Snow Canyon Park, which had some of the best lava tubes in the world. I wanted to take Jamie and Jenifer but Jamie sprained her ankle and couldn't go, but Jenifer was very excited to go. While we were climbing down into the lava tubes Chuck helped Jenifer down and it was really cool. We walked in the sand, which was very challenging; my knees were "clicking" from the strain. He could hear it and asked if I was in pain. I said, yes, but it doesn't slow me down. I was amazed that he paid that much attention to me and was concerned about how I was feeling. I never had a man be that concerned about me before, and it felt good.

As we walked, I saw a lady in the distance walking with a man and two children. I told Chuck I had a feeling that she was going to fall and break her leg. She took two steps and fell. It was obvious that she broke her leg. We were the only ones out there besides them. Jenifer and I stayed with the couple, while Chuck went back and got them help.

Sid Gets Arrested

The following week Chuck and I visited my oldest daughter, Rachel, in Salt Lake City. Jenifer had a court-ordered visitation with Sid, and my daughter, Jamie, had made plans with her friends. We packed up camping gear and headed north to visit Rachel that evening. Instead of driving home late at night we found a campground and pitched our tent. Chuck said he respected me and wouldn't make any advances. He slept in his sleeping bag and I slept in mine.

The next day, when we arrived back at the trailer and opened the door, it was trashed. Jamie said Sid had just left with Jenifer and was really mad. He knew I was with someone, and he found the divorce papers I had been putting together for court.

I told Chuck that my husband was not a nice man and that I was scared. I was very afraid for Jenifer, who was with Sid.

I thought about getting a protection order many times, but Sid was an avid hunter who loved his guns and I knew that if I did, they would take away his guns. I knew that would make him really, really mad and he'd take it out on us.

The next day at work I received a call from my soon-to-be ex-husband Sid. He said he had a loaded gun and was on his way to kill me.

I walked into the office of the Director of Nursing and told her that my daughter was sick and I needed to leave. I turned to leave, then stopped. "No," I said, "My daughter is not sick." I told her about the phone call and that I really thought he would do it. I didn't want to put the nursing home residents in harm's way. I explained to her that I could not work there anymore because I had to go into hiding.

When I got home I explained to Jamie that we were moving and could only take basic stuff. We went to Sylvia's. I told her what was happening and that I was really scared. I called my brother, who lived near Sid, to see if he could get Jenifer. He told me that Sid was drunk and had just left with Jennifer and a loaded gun.

Chuck called Sylvia to see if I was there. She told Chuck what was going on. Sylvia talked me into calling the cops. Something I had never done before because I thought it would just make things worse. Reluctantly, and in pure fear, I called the police. They told me to come to the station to file a report.

Jamie and I went to the police station. I had Jamie sit in the car to watch for her dad. If he showed up, I told her, she was to quickly come in the station and tell us. I had barely started the report when Jamie rushed in and said, "Dad's coming down the hill."

He was on his way to Sylvia's, thinking I was there. I believe that if I had been there he would have killed all of us. The cops pulled him over right in front of Sylvia's nursing home. Sid got out of the car and went toward the police. They told him to stop, but he didn't comply.

It took five cops to take him down. After they subdued him they found his loaded gun under the front seat of the car. I grabbed Jenifer and put her in my car.

They took him to jail and told me they'd keep him overnight and I could go home. The charges were drunk driving, having a loaded concealed weapon, resisting arrest, assaulting an officer, threatening bodily harm and other charges.

After Sid was arrested I went to Sylvia's to let her know that I had Jenifer and we were O.K. I was not sure where I was going to go. Sylvia and Chuck had discussed a plan for me to stay at Chuck's house until I could figure out what to do. They wanted me to get a protection order but I told them that would make matters worse. A protection order would not stop a bullet. My first instinct was to run fast and hard; to go somewhere no one knew me and start over. I kept all our identification papers in my vehicle in preparation for this day -- the day of our great escape and never to return.

The girls and I went to Chuck's apartment. We needed to go back to the trailer to get some of our stuff. We called the police to see if Sid was still in jail; they said he was. We asked them to call if they were going to release him. I was in the trailer five minutes before the police called to say that Sid had just been released. We quickly left. I knew that from that moment on my life would be completely different.

In Hiding

I no longer had a home or a job because I was too afraid to go back to work. We hid at Chuck's house, but I felt like I was in prison because we couldn't leave. We slept on the floor because Chuck's apartment was completely vacant. He had no furniture because he had recently moved to St. George from Washington state.

He called his soon-to-be ex-wife, Jodi, in Salt Lake City to see if she'd let him pick up his son, CJ and take him to the local amusement park. She said O.K., and we spent the day with Jamie, Jenifer and CJ. It felt really nice, like we were all a family. Chuck and I were best friends and our friendship deepened.

We had to drop CJ back at his mother's place. CJ threw a fit over us going camping without him. We asked his mother's permission, but she was against it at first. Then she reluctantly agreed to allow CJ to go with us.

As we drove, Jamie adjusted her seat and accidentally pulled Chuck's seat lever. His seat went all the way back. He jammed on the brakes and pulled over but said nothing.

CJ told Jamie, "Oh, you are in trouble." Jamie started crying, but Chuck had zero response. Everything stopped. My heart was racing. The kids and I were used to a man reacting with violence; we were really scared. To us, no response was the most fearful because it meant a violent eruption later on.

Chuck said everything was O.K., he just didn't know how to react. I explained that we came from a violent background and were terrified by his not responding. That was our first drama with Chuck.

When we got to Saint George the kids decided to go to the movies instead of camping. CJ finally had sisters to go to the movies with and he was excited. We dropped the kids off at the movie theater and told them to meet us after the movie outside the front door. They were told to stick together and if there was any trouble (translation: if any of Sid's family was there) they were to call me immediately.

Chuck and I went for a drive. We got out of the car and sat on a log overlooking Saint George. He put his arm around me and it made me feel safe. It was the very first time he ever touched me. A month later our friendship developed into a loving, intimate relationship.

Fighting for CJ

Chuck wanted to get custody of his son because he felt
that CJ's mother was not a fit mother. I suggested he
get a psychological evaluation on his son. His attorney
recommended someone, and we were able to have it done that
same day. Chuck was very nervous about going to court.

The next day, after several hours of negotiation, Jodi finally
gave up the custody battle. Their attorneys agreed on the
terms of the divorce and custody.

CJ came to live with us, his new family. He was happy
to have sisters and a true family. We all returned to Saint
George with one more battle to fight.

Divorcing Sid

The girls and I were still staying with Chuck when Sid agreed
to let us go by the house and pick up our personal property.
When Chuck, CJ, the girls and I arrived and began looking
for our stuff, Sid got increasingly angry. We could see that he
was about to lose it, so we left.

He followed us, but we were able to outrun him and hid for
the night. We were too terrified to go back to Chuck's place,
so we slept in the car.

The next day, Sid called the kids and asked to talk to me. I could tell he had not been drinking yet. He said he was sorry, and would do whatever I wanted regarding the divorce. I could hear the regret in his voice as we discussed how to split up our assets. I would get my car and two houses and he would get one house and some personal property, like tools, the truck, equipment, etc.

Soon after that, we signed the papers and quit claim deeds for the houses. Even though it seemed the divorce was going O.K. we lived every day in fear. Having Chuck around made us feel a little safer; he was twice as big as Sid, so we thought he could protect us.

I Marry Chuck & We Move to AZ

As soon as my divorce from Sid was final, Chuck asked me to marry him. We were married on Friday, November 13, 1998. The ceremony performed in my home by Bishop Baron. The mayor, the mayor's husband, my family, Chuck's grandparents, and Brother Beard attended. They were all happy and supportive and said this man was the one. As my aunt said one night at dinner, he's a keeper. Everyone was happy that I now had a real man in my life – a nice man who would take care of us and always be there for us.

We moved into my house in Fredonia, Arizona and lived the most normal life the girls and I had ever lived before. My kids had two parents who got along and a new brother. This was the first time in their lives they had a normal family, a family they were proud of. The kids were happy and seemed well adjusted. With Chuck everything flowed nicely.

The Honeymoon

The night before we left on our honeymoon the kids decorated the car; it was so cute. We drove down to California where Chuck wanted to introduce his new bride to his grandfather. He hadn't seen him in several years and didn't have his phone number, but he knew where he lived.

When his grandfather opened the door he was excited to see Chuck and meet his new wife. He welcomed me into the family and told us many stories, as only old men can do. He was a charming old man who had been a fighter pilot in WWII. It was fun talking with him.

After spending the day with grandpa we continued on our journey. We stayed at a cheap hotel in Anaheim, California. I noticed that the window coverings were out of place and there was a smell of bleach in the room, which seemed odd. Chuck and I fixed the curtains and then turned on the TV. There was no picture, so we turned it off. Chuck went to complain about the TV to the front office and I took a shower. When Chuck returned he said they were going to send someone to fix it. I tried the TV again, and it worked.

After watching TV for about an hour, we heard a loud knock at the door. Chuck asked who it was and the voice behind the door said, "It's the cable guy." Chuck told him we didn't need him anymore. The guy knocked again. Chuck asked him what he wanted, and a voice said, "It's the cable guy." Chuck again told him we don't want it. The knock came again and this time Chuck opened the door. No one was there, even though we had heard him knock just a few seconds earlier. We were discussing how odd that was, when the TV shut off by itself. Chuck tried to turn the TV back on, but it would not go on. So, we turned off the lights and went to bed. We had just fallen asleep when the TV came back on by itself. We thought that was pretty creepy and unplugged the TV set.

The next day I noticed that the cable to the TV was not the original cable, but had been replaced. That, the smell of bleach, the mismatched curtains and the invisible cable guy, made us curious about what else might be odd in the room. We decided to unmake the bed. We flipped the mattress over and the other side was bloody and had many knife marks through it. It was really creepy. When we checked out, the receptionist looked at the key and said, "Oh. They're not supposed to rent out that room." We asked her what happened in the room, but she refused to tell us. From then on we called it our haunted honeymoon. I found it intriguing, but Chuck didn't agree.

We continued on to San Diego and toured the old ship museums. For amusement, I made up stories about what happened on the ships and pretended to be the tour guide who was a ghost. I could hardly wait to tell the kids about it when we got home. I knew they'd think it was cool.

After that we went on a cruise to Mexico. It was Chuck's first cruise. When we got to our cabin there was a sign on the door that said 'Happy Honeymoon *Michael* and Chuck.' Chuck thought it was funny but it irritated me.

When we got home I told the kids, and Rachel, who was taking care of them while we were gone, about our haunted honeymoon. They were excited to hear about it and thought it was pretty cool.

Xmas Surprise

Chuck quickly became a very good stepfather and role model for my kids. Our kids welcomed him as a parent and were excited about our new family. We did everything together: camping, fishing, kayaking, sailing, and had family story nights. We took the kids on their first scuba diving adventure in Pocatello, Idaho, during a Gold Wing Road Riders motorcycle rally. They were so excited about this new adventure and doing it as a family.

After returning from our honeymoon we spent our first Christmas together as a family. Chuck's parents decided to join us since they were unable to attend the wedding. They gave each of the kids a gift, which was a little airplane made out of thin wood.

Then they gave me a box and said, "Here, we got you something." This was not only my Christmas gift, they said, but also my wedding present. I opened it, not knowing what to expect. In the box was sexy lingerie – something like a "teddy." It was dirty and stained and was obviously "used."

I was so embarrassed. My new in-laws gave me used underwear! I quickly put it back in the box and thanked them. After they left, I showed Chuck that it was dirty and used. He was embarrassed and baffled that his parents gave his new bride used underwear.

Kids' School Drama

Jenifer and CJ were in the same fifth-grade classroom. Jenifer was upset about their teacher using the F word and the B word while reading stories. I told the children that since I had no evidence of the teacher saying these words, it was not my place to confront the teacher. They would need to deal with this problem in their own way.

A couple of days later, I got a phone call from the school. Both children were in the principal's office. The word 'slander' was mentioned and the principal wanted to meet with us immediately, without the children. The principal escorted us to a room where the teacher was waiting. Jenifer had written a petition to the school board accusing the teacher of using bad language. There were signatures from five other students on the petition. When I questioned Jenifer, she said the teacher's aide had prevented them from talking to the principal, so she took the next logical step of going to the school board.

They asked us what we intended to do about our children's bad behavior. I said that since we weren't there in the classroom, we don't know what happened or didn't happen. The following year that teacher resigned.

This was one of many incidents at that school involving the kids. One time the school called saying Jenifer's teacher claimed she was drawing pornographic pictures and to come to the school immediately. When we arrived at the principal's office, the teacher was waiting. She showed me the picture Jenifer drew and called it pornographic.

Jenifer had been an artist since she was two and drew pictures all the time. The picture was of a lady at the beach lying face down on a towel, with her bikini top lying next to her. I told the teacher I would not be ashamed to show that picture to anyone and, in fact, it was very good artwork. They insisted it was pornographic because the lady was not wearing her bathing suit top. I thought they were picking on her because of the letter she wrote to the school board the previous year. I told the principal I thought they were conducting a 'witch hunt' against my daughter. That was the end of that it.

Our Second Christmas Together

I have fond memories of our second Christmas together. We invited my brother Mike and my sister Leslie and their families to share Christmas with us. Mike had three kids and Leslie had one son. Before our family party I loaded the kids into the car and gave each one a gift with an anonymous card saying, "No one should be left out at Christmas." I told the kids to each pick a neighbor and give them their "secret" gift. The idea was to spread the spirit of Christmas. I figured that if everyone who got a gift from us gave someone else a gift, everyone in town would have a gift by the time Christmas arrived. The kids went up to the houses of their choice, put the gift on the porch, knocked on the door and ran away.

The kids thought this was fun and wanted to do it again the following night. CJ was excited to give his friend from school a gift. So, we headed out again and went to the house where he said his friend lived. CJ put the gift on the porch, knocked on the door and ran. However, it was the wrong house. This big guy comes out with a shot gun. With the door opened, we could see a big confederate flag in the background. He saw the gift on the porch and yelled back at us, "Thank you."

CJ never had a Christmas like ours. We had a family tradition of not buying gifts. The rule was: you can find one or make one, but not buy one. The kids found stuff in their rooms, wrapped it up and gave them to their cousins for Christmas. CJ said it was the best Christmas he ever had.

The Family's First Summer Vacation

That summer we went on our first family vacation to Yosemite National Park in California. We drove through Area 51 and the kids looked around for flying saucers. When we got to the campsite we pitched our tents. The kids had the big tent and Chuck and I shared the small tent. We fixed dinner as a family and told camping stories. We were so tired, we went to bed without cleaning up. We were told no one had seen a bear in that campground for five years.

Jenifer was mad at Jamie and CJ for teasing her, so she decided to sleep outside instead of inside the kids' tent. That night, Chuck woke me up and asked me if I wanted to see a bear. I looked out of our tent and there was a bear about three feet from us. I covered my head and Chuck made some noise, and the bear ran away.

We checked on the kids and woke them up to tell them we saw a bear. We looked around our campsite and noticed that our ice chest was missing. We got our flashlights and went looking for our ice chest. While we searched, we spotted a bear behind a tree drinking someone's Yoo-hoo. We found our ice chest. It had bear teeth marks on it and everything in our ice chest was gone. As we carried it back to our campsite, Jenifer told us that she had been sleeping with her head next to the ice chest.

My Nephew Chris

One day in 2001 I got a call from paramedics informing me that my sister Leslie's son had been found dead. It was horrible news. It made a huge void in my life; he was my cutie-pie Chris.

Chuck was emotionally distant, so I didn't get any support from him. Once again, I was relied on to be the strong, responsible one of the family. Rachel came and stayed with me. She knew I was going through hell and wanted to be there for me.

Chuck was disconnected and had nothing to say about the situation, except that he was sorry. I felt Chuck could not relate to the way I loved and adored Chris. I married this strong, handsome dude any woman would be proud to have, yet his behavior showed that he was not like the rest of us.

I began to think that Chuck was not really married to me emotionally and that he may have had some other reason for marrying me. During that time, my sister Leslie also expressed concern about Chuck's behavior.

We had a simple celebration of Chris' life instead of mourning his death. I wanted him to stay forever, but I knew I had to let him go. When I thought about Chris I knew he was with me in my heart.

Jenifer and Chuck

Jenifer, Chuck and CJ joined the Civil Air Patrol together. They attended weekly meetings and did mock search and recovery missions. When the Columbia space shuttle was destroyed, the Civil Air Patrol in Saint George was part of the search and recovery mission in the Utah area. NASA thought parts of the shuttle may have landed in Utah so we were all looking for parts, but didn't find any.

Chuck was a role model to Jenifer and I think she joined the military to make him proud. They shared many of the same interests. They worked on art projects and talked about books and movies. He made her feel special and they could talk about anything. One time they rode on his motorcycle to the Grand Canyon. Jenifer had suffered so much with her real dad, it was awesome to see them become friends.

Pick Up Truck

Chuck had always wanted a pick up truck. We had looked at dealerships but we never bought anything. Chuck had bad credit, so he couldn't buy it without me.

One day I suggested we get a truck, and he happily agreed. I looked online and called dealerships looking for a Toyota Tacoma five-speed. I found one in Las Vegas for a good price and zero financing. Chuck was so excited; we went to pick it up that night.

The next day we ordered a camper shell and he asked me where I wanted to go with the new truck. I said I wanted to go to a hot spring. We went online and got the GPS coordinates for Father Escalante's Hot Spring in Utah and put them into our GPS unit. I packed up the truck in case we got stuck somewhere; some of the roads on the way were not paved.

We went onto a dirt road and drove for an hour. At the end of the dirt road we made a turn, according to the GPS instructions.

After about 5 miles we saw someone walking up ahead of us. We had not seen anyone that day. We stopped and rolled down the window. It was an older man. He walked with a limp and he had no jacket or water. Of course, we offered him a ride.

He said he was trying to take a short cut home when his car got stuck in a mud hole. He had been walking for hours and had not seen anyone to help him.

He asked where we were going; we told him we were looking for a hot spring. We gave him water and he drank half a gallon. We came to a crossroads that said hot spring one way and the town the other way. The man said he didn't mind going to the hot spring with us.

When we got there, we found only a mud hole with cows all around it. Needless to say, we did not stay. We drove to the closest town and dropped the man off.

He said we saved his life. He thought this was the day he was going to die. I felt part of the reason we bought the truck at that time was to save this man's life. We wouldn't have been out there on those desolate roads in a regular car. The man was very grateful.

After that, Chuck wanted to take a little vacation to Washington State. We packed up the truck and dropped the kids at the Civil Air Patrol training camp on the way to Washington.

We had a good time, getting to know each other without the rest of the family around. We went kayaking in the San Juan Islands and camped there for a couple of days. We went whale watching and saw an Orca. We loved camping with the new truck and discussed camping all summer long once the kids were grown.

Chuck mentioned that he would like to move back to Washington. During the trip, we looked around for homes for sale to see what was available. We could not relocate right away because the kids were in school. I liked Washington but I was concerned about the weather being too cold for me. But, I would do anything for my sweetheart and was happy to move if it made him happy. After that, moving to Washington became an obsession with Chuck.

The Kids Leave Home

The following year CJ decided he wanted to move in with his aunt in Billings, Montana, and finish high school there.

Jenifer decided to join the Job Corps like her two sisters had done. She felt high school was a waste of her time and wanted to finish school sooner. When she turned sixteen and was eligible for Job Corps, she signed up. I hated to see her go, but I let her make her own choice.

I expected my kids to live at home for a few more years, so I was very surprised, and not at all prepared, for their decisions to leave.

This left Chuck and I with no kids around and time to start our life as a couple.

Chuck and I Move to Washington

In October of 2004 we purchased a cabin on Harstine Island in Western Washington. The cabin was in need of repair. The owner passed away and no one was there to take care of it. There weren't even any steps up to the front door. We knew it would take a lot of work, but we had plenty of time to fix it up.

I was glad to leave Utah where I had to constantly be on guard because of my ex-husband's threats. Now, I didn't have to worry about Sid. It was a very peaceful place and was more relaxed than I had been in a long time.

We were excited to have the cabin ready for the kids to come for Thanksgiving. All the kids came. The wildlife came up close to the cabin and everyone had a great time. After Thanksgiving we continued to work on the cabin to make it our home.

After moving to Washington, Chuck seemed different. I wondered if it was because of the big changes in our lifestyle.

In January of the following year, Chuck wanted to see a counselor for a mental illness he suffered during his time in the military. The first time he went to the counselor he behaved as though he didn't want to go. He finally got up the courage to go into the counselor's office.

He said the counseling was covered by his insurance, but I found out later it was not. He was paying hundreds of dollars a month on his own to see the counselor. This extra cost was a burden on our household, but the sessions made a huge difference in our life. He talked about the doctor a lot, saying this doctor was different from all of the doctors he had seen previously.

Chuck became more and more distant from me, but was making friends online in nearby Tacoma. It made me wonder if his reasons for wanting to move to Washington had nothing to do with our life together. I was willing to move for the sake of his happiness, even though I was uncomfortable being so far away from my kids. All I could do was visit them frequently. I visited the kids in Utah every other month. Chuck always encouraged me to stay with them as long as possible.

A year later, when I returned home from a visit with the kids, Chuck had shaved off his mustache. He said he won the lottery and decided to get laser hair removal so that when we traveled he wouldn't have to bring his razor. He became more secretive during that time, but I had no idea why.

A year after Chuck had been seeing this doctor, we were driving home from an appointment when he told me to stop the car. He said he had something very important to tell me and it was very hard to say.

He had gotten a new diagnosis -- he had gender dysphoria. I
had no idea what that was. I told him I did not understand.
He told me this story about how he was supposed to be
a twin, and his twin would have been a girl. His mom,
pregnant with twins, lost the girl early on in the womb. He
said he took on her soul as well as his own, so he was actually
two different people in the same body. This did not make
sense to me. I asked if that meant he wanted to be a female.
He said no, he just felt he should have been born a girl.

I was very concerned about his mental health, and thought he
might need to be on medication. He said there was no cure
for this disorder, and he would have to work through it with
the counselor. Maybe taking hormones would make him feel
better as a person, he said.

I was devastated by what he said and had no idea how my life
was going to be from then on. I felt as though my whole life
was a lie. It was a horrible feeling and I had no one to talk to
about it. In the past I always thought I could run away from
problems but this time I thought there was no way out.

I had put so much money into our house, I had nothing left.
I realized that our move to Washington was not about us
retiring together.

I came up with a survival plan. I would enroll in massage
school and become a licensed massage practitioner. I had
always enjoyed giving neck and shoulder massages to family
members and even to a few teachers at school.

There were three massage schools in my area and I wanted the best one. I went to each of the schools and received a massage from one of their qualified students. I chose Alexander's school in Tacoma. I signed up and paid a deposit right away.

On my first day of massage school they handed me a stack of books on subjects of like: anatomy, physiology, pathology, massage theory, etc. I said, "What is this?" I knew nothing about academics or how to study. It's a good thing I didn't know ahead of time that studying books was part of the curriculum, or I probably would not have enrolled. But, I was determined to get my license. As it turned out, I did very well in all of my courses.

McKinlee

While I was still in massage school, in April of 2006, my daughter Jamie, who was pregnant with my first granddaughter, McKinlee, went into labor. I took a short break from school and took the next flight to St. George to be with my daughter.

When I got to the hospital, McKinlee was in the neonatal intensive care unit on a respirator. It brought back painful memories of my son, Curtis. The doctors said she needed help breathing. After 24 hours on the respirator, we were able to take her home. A few hours later I noticed that her skin looked more yellow than when we left the hospital. I became even more concerned a little while later, when she looked even more jaundiced.

There was a loud knock at the door. When Jamie answered the door, there were three police officers telling her that the hospital had contacted the police because they had the wrong phone number for Jamie and couldn't get in touch with her. The hospital wanted us to bring the baby back immediately because her jaundice was at a dangerous level.

She spent another 24 hours at the hospital for monitoring and tests until we were able to bring her home again for good. Today McKinlee is the smartest, cutest little redhead I've ever seen and a huge joy to our family.

I returned to massage school and was soon caught up in all my classes.

PART SIX

The Blog

I returned home from massage school one day in November, 2006, and went to the computer. There was a blog on the screen called "Amber B's Blog." I had never seen that name before. I soon realized that it was my husband talking about how he hated me and thought I was going to kill myself. That was a big surprise since I was very happy and had never been suicidal. My heart was pounding as I read. He was counting down the days until he got rid of me. He also talked about some man with a tight-fitting shirt that he thought was really hot.

I was shocked and devastated. I couldn't even finish reading the blog because I was so upset. When he got home that night from jury duty in Shelton, I asked him about the blog. He told me that it was just a story he was writing and not about our lives.

He got angry when I questioned him. I asked if he was gay. He said, "definitely not." – but, I didn't believe him. This was our first fight.

That weekend, my daughter Rachel came up for Thanksgiving. I was able to act as if everything was normal, but there were a lot of questions swirling around in my head.

The Big Wind Storm

On December 15, 2006 there was a big wind storm that knocked the power out for weeks in most of Western Washington. The night before, we had packed up the truck for a trip to see the kids in Utah for the holidays. The morning after the wind storm we went outside and found that a tree had fallen on my car; but the truck was not damaged.

Chuck had not been talking to me that morning. All of a sudden, he got in the truck and took off with all our stuff. He left me alone in the house with no electricity. The temperature dropped to 34 degrees inside the house at night. I spent two nights in the house waiting for him to return. My kids asked me to get on the next plane to Saint George to stay with them.

I had no idea where my husband was; he didn't answer my calls. I left Chuck a message that I was going to go ahead and see the children for Christmas. I bought a one-way ticket, thinking he might drive to St. George and I'd be able to ride back to Washington with him.

I felt abandoned. I cried for hours. I didn't want to burden my children with the details of the situation. I thought no one could understand the hell I was going through. How could this happen to me? *This is not my life*.

My entire body hurt. I could barely move. Jenifer met me at the airport and took me straight to the emergency room. I told her I had been through hell, but couldn't talk about it. My leg muscles were twitching and I was in a lot of pain. I found out that emotional pain can cause severe physical pain in one's body. I ended up telling my daughter what happened. I felt my whole life was falling apart.

I told the kids about the blog. It felt like my life was out of my control. They wanted me to move back to Saint George and stay with them. But, I had six more weeks of massage school and wanted to finish.

Out of the blue, Chuck called me to ask where his birth certificate was. I told him where it was, but couldn't bring myself to ask why he wanted it. He said he had been in Mountain Home, Idaho, getting counseling from a preacher and that he felt better.

He wasn't sure if he could make it to St. George for Christmas because he had some things he had to do. I was very upset and said I didn't understand. He said he'd explain later, though I probably wouldn't understand anyway. He agreed to pick me up at the airport when I got back. It was the worst Christmas I ever had.

Airport Pick-Up

I waited for Chuck outside Sea-Tac airport. When I saw
the truck pull up, I reached down to pick up my bag off the
sidewalk. When I looked up, he jumped out of the truck
wearing a bright red wig, pierced earrings, a dress and high
heels. I was horrified!

It was obvious he was a man wearing a dress and high heels.
I'm one who likes to blend into a crowd, not stand out. I
could not breathe. I was not prepared for this. This man,
who had been my best friend and husband, was now someone
I did not know at all.

Before I could say anything, he handed me his driver's
license and said, "Look. My name is Amber and the state of
Washington recognizes me as a female." From that moment
on, Amber was my living nightmare.

I got into the truck and didn't say anything except, *This is not
my life.* He did all the talking. I was told to refer to him only
as Amber. He said he didn't want to be with me anymore,
because I was not a lesbian, and he only wanted to be with a
lesbian. Then he said he had packed up all my stuff and put
it in a storage trailer on a vacant piece of property I owned.
Hearing all this was a very big shock. The trailer was not a
livable space. I was still in school full-time, had no job or
money and my car couldn't go very far.

81

On the road driving back we stopped at a McDonald's. I walked in hoping no one would see me or think I was with this man wearing a dress. This was the person I was supposed to spend my life with. I couldn't eat. I was sick to my stomach.

He insisted on going inside instead of using the drive-thru. I guess he wanted to show off his new wig and earrings. He was proud of what he had done and wanted other people to know about it. He was like a peacock flashing its feathers. He was probably thinking, 'Look at me - I'm a hot woman.' But, I was thinking he looked like a freak.

I went into the bathroom just to get away from him. I had to remind myself to keep breathing. I didn't want anyone to know how devastated I was. Everyone depended on me being the "stable" one. I had to be strong. Besides, I was too embarrassed to tell anyone about it.

He said he wanted me out of his life and that I had to find another place or he wouldn't pay the bills. Then he added, "I know how important your credit is to you."

Up to this point I could control my emotions, but now I felt I was about to go out of my mind. The abuse I suffered with Sid was really bad, but this was worse because it was mentally and emotionally devastating. My whole life was turned upside down.

When Chuck told me he was no longer my husband, it was very traumatic. I was in love with him and wanted to believe he married me because he loved me. Now I realized he just used me as a stepping stone to womanhood. It was hard to admit that I had left one abusive relationship for another.

Looking back on our life together, I could see that he was thinking about financing his sex change surgery for a long time. I recalled that shortly after Chuck and I got married, he expressed concern that if I died, my girls would kick him out and he'd have no place to go. He wanted me to write a will leaving him some of my property. I refused, because I wanted my kids to have it all. Even though all I had was two houses and a car, it was more than he would ever have without me. He wanted my property to pay for his dream of living as a woman.

I also realized that he wanted to move to Washington so I'd be farther away from my family, making it easier for him to control me and my assets. He had no intention of spending the rest of his life with me. He needed to get rid of me so he could pursue his goals.

I berated myself, over and over, for missing so many red flags. I did not want to admit to my kids that my life was now out of control and that Chuck not the person we all thought he was.

Losing My Home/Telling the Kids

I took my sleeping bag over to the lot with the trailer on it. I stayed there with no heat or water. I woke up the next morning feeling completely alone. My kids were grown and had their own families; I didn't want to burden them with my problems. I stayed in the trailer a couple of nights, but the cold got unbearable.

I spent New Year's Eve with a friend named Jack in Shelton, Washington. He was the only person I knew in the area at the time. We partied pretty hard at his house that night – I just wanted to forget my life. I'm not sure how much I drank, but I passed out on his couch. I woke up in the morning with a big black German Shepard's face in my face. All I could think was, *This is not my life*. I got up, got in my car and drove away.

I needed somewhere to stay, so I drove to my Aunt Karon's house in Tacoma. It was January 1, 2007. When she answered the door, I started crying. I told her I couldn't talk about it right then, but I had no where to live. I had to stay in Washington because I had six more weeks of massage school.

I told her Chuck didn't love me anymore. She could not believe it. She really liked Chuck. Everyone in my family liked Chuck and knew we would be together forever. Later, I was able to tell her the story. She was shocked. She said she had an RV I could use until I finished school.

84

My back hurt so much every day I could barely get through school. The owner of the school and his assistant John were the only ones who knew how I was suffering.

My children took the news about Chuck very hard, especially Jenifer. She said that he was more than a stepfather to her, he was her best friend.

When Jamie was told about Chuck she took it very hard and cried hysterically. She called her husband at work and said, "My mom and Chuck... You need to come home now." Her husband thought we had died. He told his boss he had to go home because something happened to Jamie's mom.

I cannot describe the emotional devastation and heartache my children and I went through. I felt so bad for them having to see their mom so emotionally upset. I could not imagine seeing my own mother so devastated.

My kids suffered a lot with Sid, but this was far worse because it broke their trust in someone they loved and looked up to. Now he was gone and there was no chance for any of us to say goodbye.

When I called my brother Mike to tell him about Chuck, he thought I was making it up. Later he told me that it took him a month to believe me, but still wasn't 100% sure I was telling the truth. He and Chuck had been very good friends. He was like the brother Mike never had. They did all kinds of "guy stuff" together – fishing, boating, building things, etc. Mike was very upset over losing his friend.

My heart was broken. I had lost the love of my life, my best friend, and my husband. I could not understand why he was doing this. It would have been easier for me if he had just died, because then at least I could have grieved the loss and had some closure.

Transgender Research

Earlier that year, Chuck asked me to attend a transgender support group meeting. I thought it might help me understand what was happening, so I agreed to go.

The next week I attended a meeting at the Rainbow Center in Tacoma. I sat and listened, but felt very uncomfortable with Chuck/Amber sitting across from me.

Everyone introduced themselves. I said I was the wife of a member and was there to find out how my life could change so quickly. Chuck/Amber introduced himself/herself as Michelle's husband.

The people at the meeting were nice to me. One of them, Gwen and her friend, Sharon, invited me to a potluck at the following week's meeting. I called my friend Jerry, a genetic female, and asked her to go with me. She didn't mind going, she said, because she, too, wanted to find out how my life turned out this way.

Gwen and Sharon welcomed us to the potluck. Gwen liked how I interacted with her dog, Sasha. I felt a connection to Gwen because of her dog and volunteered to dog sit for her. She called me the next week and asked if I'd watch her dog. That's how Gwen and I became good friends. I thought of Gwen as a regular person, just like Jerry and me. I felt as though she was my girlfriend and not a man. She also gave me the book, "My Husband Betty." I wondered if the reading material on transgender people was very limited since two members of the group gave me the same book.

My friend Jerry and I became close friends with Gwen and Sharon. We would meet and help them pick out clothes. I thought it might help me understand why my husband made the choice to live as a woman. But, I still could not understand any of it. I was as confused as ever. Gwen became a good friend and an important support person for me.

Paying For Chuck's Sex-Change Surgery

In February of 2007, Chuck offered to buy me a travel trailer, pay the rent for the space and all the bills. In exchange, he wanted me to sign this one piece of paper – a bank application for a line of credit on the Harstine Island house. The purpose of the loan, he said, was to wind down the marriage.

I asked, 'How do I know you won't use this money for your sex-change operation?"

"Rest assured," he said, "I can't get a sex change anytime soon. I have to live full-time as a woman for one year before they'll let me do that." Good, I thought, that gives me time to get my new life together and get divorced from him before he changes into a woman.

Chuck bought me an RV out of "the goodness of his heart," he said. I guess he didn't want to think of himself as a bad transgender person since he had made me homeless. But, it made me feel he really did love me, despite everything. "Even though I'm a tranny," he said, "I'll make sure you're taken care of." At least with the trailer I had my own place to sleep at night.

In May, I ran into one of Chuck's transgender friends. She told me that Chuck was planning to go to Bangkok, Thailand soon to have a sex change operation. I knew instantly that Chuck was going to pay for it with the line of credit on the house – the house I had paid for all by myself. That's how I found out I was the one financing his sex change.

I confronted Chuck about what she said. He denied it, saying the loan was only to wind down our marriage. He was lying, of course.

As it turned out, instead of having to wait a year, somehow he was able to schedule his operation after only five months. He must have convinced the counselor who told him he was a woman in the first place, to sign the papers for the surgery.

He pretended the line of credit on the house was to wind down the marriage. But, the truth was he wanted the money to fix what he called his "birth defect." A few weeks later, Chuck went to Thailand for his sex change operation.

Besides the loan on the house, Chuck had made several fraudulent charges on one of my credit cards, including a check payable to Amber for $5,500. He bought a new Harley-Davidson and joined a motorcycle group called, Dykes on Bikes.

I had previously removed Chuck's name from my credit card account when we were separated, but I found out later that Chuck had re-added his name to the card, and also added the name Amber. Chuck had committed fraud to make his sex change possible.

I Finish Massage School

As soon as I finished school, I applied for the national licensing exam and asked for the earliest possible opening. It usually takes months to schedule the exam, but I was so desperate to get my license, I called the office every day asking if there had been any cancellations. Miraculously, someone did cancel and I was able to get licensed in two weeks. I was still in agonizing back and leg pain.

Near the end of the school, one of my fellow students asked if I would exchange massages. I said only if she would let me direct her to the areas of my body that were in the most pain. She agreed. As she worked on my back I told her to put as much pressure as she could along the sciatica nerve in my glutes. It was excruciatingly painful.

I thought, this is really a "pain in the ass." In that moment I knew that the physical pain in my butt represented the emotional and psychological "pain in my ass," Amber. I realized that my anger and sadness was causing the hellish pain in my body – a revelation that has benefited me immensely in my massage practice. I made a decision, then and there, to consciously let go of those negative emotions. When I got up off the massage table, my back pain was gone.

Amber and Tami

Before his sex-change surgery in May, Chuck/Amber had met someone on Yahoo named Tami. As soon as Amber got back from Thailand, she moved to Pendleton, Oregon to live with Tami as a lesbian.

On July 1, I called Amber to tell her I was going to have a party at the Harstine Island house on the 4th of July. She said she had already invited all of her friends to the house for the 4th. Since I didn't want my friends' children around that situation, I cancelled my party.

I went out to the house by myself on the 4th of July to get my kayak. One of Amber's friends helped me load the kayak on top of my car. Amber and her lesbian girlfriend were down at the beach. When they saw me they started kissing passionately. It was very upsetting. I did not see Amber kissing Tami, but my husband Chuck kissing Tami. It was obviously done just to hurt me – I guess he thought I hadn't suffered enough torment – he had to do one last thing.

As I walked away, Amber asked, "What's wrong?" I didn't say anything, I just kept walking.

Locked Out of My House

After their party, I moved back into the Harstine house. I didn't think it would be a problem since Amber had moved everything to Pendleton. I paid the taxes and the last year's homeowner dues that were delinquent. Several months later, when Amber found out I moved into the house she was angry. I didn't understand why, since the house was sitting empty.

In late August, 2007, I returned home from work and found myself locked out of my house. I knew it was Amber's doing, so I went to the sheriff's station for help. They told me that someone named Amber, giving the Harstine house as their residence, had filed a Protection Order against me.

The Protection Order also claimed that Amber was a battered woman and I was the batterer. She had used my abuse experiences with Sid and replaced my name with Amber's in the report. When I saw the protection order I got really mad – I was ready to fight back.

Protection Order

I went to see the commissioner who signed the protection order and told him the facts: Amber had moved from the Harstine house to Pendleton, Oregon last May, that I hadn't seen her since then, and I certainly did not batter her. The commissioner was upset at being lied to and immediately threw out the protection order. That began a big battle with Amber and the court system.

I immediately filed a restraining order against Amber. Amber and Tami were at the courthouse about the protection order, so the commissioner called a hearing on my restraining order for the same day. After a short hearing, the Commissioner granted me the restraining order to keep Amber from going to the Harstine Island house.

A few days later, Amber hired an attorney, Paul, who filed a motion to reconsider both the protection order and the restraining order. We went before a judge, but she couldn't make a ruling at that time. She left my restraining order in place, and set a hearing on October 31, 2007 for Amber's protection order. In the meantime, she granted me permission to return to the Harstine Island house and gave Amber a temporary protection order until the hearing.

During the hearing on the protection order, Amber's friends and girlfriend, Tami, testified against me. Since Amber had used the discrimination card before, I asked my transgender friend Gwen, to observe the hearing. If there was an appeal on the basis of discrimination, I'd have her opinion on the fairness of the hearing. Later, because she supported me, she was scorned by her transgender friends and forced to resign as president of the group.

I was embarrassed going to court with this 6' 2" man wearing a dress and claiming to be a battered woman. We were referred to as Ms. and Ms. by the commissioner, who got confused at times, calling me Amber, adding insult to injury. A court official told me people were coming in to just see the show. The court room was packed.

Amber's attorney turned the protection order into a division of property issue, stating that Amber was living at the house on Harstine Island. It was clear to me that the protection order was really about Amber wanting to take possession of the Harstine house. In the past Amber had threatened to destroy me financially if she did not get the house.

When I confronted Amber with the fact that she lived in Oregon, not in Washington, as she claimed, the judge asked Amber if she had an out of state driver's license. This was crucial, because in order to get an Oregon license, she had to surrender her Washington license and prove she was an Oregon resident.

Amber took a long time to answer 'no.' The judge asked her, "Are you sure? Remember you are under oath." Then her attorney told her to tell the truth. She stuttered a while, then admitted she had lied to the judge about her license and where she lived. Amber's protection order was dismissed.

The restraining order I obtained was dismissed because the commissioner failed to follow the proper procedure. I filed another restraining order because I knew that without it, Amber would try to lock me out of the house again.

During the new restraining order hearing, the commissioner, for no apparent reason other then he was sick of us, turned things around and gave *me* a 30-day notice to move out of the house. Perhaps he was confused again, who knows. The house stayed empty and I stayed in the RV for the next year.

I moved my trailer to an RV park near Tacoma. There was a bar right across the street from the park. On Tuesdays the bar had two tacos for a buck and tequila Jell-O shots for two bucks. The perfect dinner, I thought, two tacos and ten tequila shots.

I noticed two men sitting together at the bar. One of them was crying. I asked him what was wrong. He said his wife left him and was now a lesbian and he was devastated. I took another shot of tequila, looked at him and said, "Big deal, so your wife's a lesbian. My husband became a lesbian, and then got a sex-change operation, and I had to pay for it." I don't know if the guy believed me, but he gave me a strange look and stopped crying.

PART SEVEN

Loneliness

I came out of an abusive relationship thinking I had found love at first sight. Instead I found Chuck and Amber. I guess I was an easy target.

I felt disgusted and embarrassed about his sex change. I avoided telling people I met about him. I referred to Chuck as the person I used to be married to, or the person I was getting divorced from, never as my "ex." I didn't want anyone to know that a transsexual person temporarily took over my life.

I joined e-harmony and met Matt, who had a professional job in Seattle. We became close and I felt a strong connection with him. However, Matt was borderline abusive in how he talked to me. I could not see myself with someone who made me feel uneasy. I was no longer that submissive woman and wasn't going to put up with any type of abuse. I broke it off with him right away. This was the first time it was easy to just walk away.

I was lonely and lost once again.

Desperate For Friendship

I was so desperate for friendship I went to the notorious Craigslist personal ads. I arranged to meet a man at a local pub. I went early and got two shots of tequila (liquid courage).

Before he arrived, I made friends with a man at the bar named Bobby. He and his friends sang love songs to me. Then the Craigslist person walked in. He bought me two more shots of tequila, making it four, which was not a good thing.

We started playing pool. He beat me two times and got me two more shots of tequila. He challenged me to another game, bragging how he had kicked my ass. There was no way I would allow that to happen again.

He shot in all the balls except for two, and said, "See, I will beat you."

I said, "I don't think so," and looked around the room for help. I asked this little older man if he would shoot my balls in for me. He said, "Of course, honey." I gave him my pool stick, walked over to my "date" and said, "I'm going to kick *your* ass now."

The little old man shot all my balls and the 8 ball in and I won. I had six shots of tequila by then and felt very brave. I bragged about kicking his ass after all. He was really upset and went over to the old man and said, "Lets take it outside." The bouncer told him to leave.

The guy said to me, " Bitch, you got me 86'd out of the bar."

I was afraid to walk out of the place by myself, thinking he was waiting for me. So, I listened to the men singing love songs until the bar closed at 2 a.m. Bobby gave me a ride home. I laid down on my bed and thought, *This is not my life!* How did I go from being a happy housewife to a bar hag.

The next morning, I packed up my car with camping equipment and my dog and headed to the mountains to start my life over again.

I found the perfect campsite and set up my tent; then took a walk around the campground. I saw a man sitting alone by his campfire. I asked if he had a beer, and he gave me one. He told me he was Polish and from New York, but was moving to California for a new job. He said he had been traveling across the country for three weeks and I was the friendliest person he had met. I thought, and I'm the loneliness person, too.

He invited me to stay for dinner and cooked up some polish sausage. By the end of the evening we had drunk all his beer. I returned to my tent very intoxicated, hoping to wake up from my nightmare. I got up early the next morning and said, *This is not my life.*

I headed back to Tacoma. When I got my cell phone service back, there were multiple text messages from the Craigslist guy blaming me for him being 86'd out of his local bar.

I decided I had to change the way I was meeting men. No more E-harmony or Craigslist personals. I found a singles group called Events and Adventures. I had to do something. I felt totally out of control at that point in my life.

Attending activities with Events and Adventures showed me that it was O.K. to be single. I felt more in control of my life and saw that there were lots of people out there who had never been married.

The Divorce

Amber refused to settle the divorce, so I had to go to court and have a judge settle it. Amber wanted half of everything I owned. The whole thing was difficult and confusing and seemed unreal. I married a man named Chuck, but now was divorcing a woman named Amber.

During the trial Amber was caught in a number of lies, like claiming she paid for my property in Fredonia, Arizona.

It took the judge several weeks to come to a decision. They set a time for us to come back for the reading of the final divorce decree.

During the reading of the final decree, I sat next to my attorney and cried the whole time. I felt very sad about the whole mess, especially about losing my husband, whom I loved. Chuck no longer existed in my mind; he was now Amber, a person I did not know.

The night before I had to go back to the courthouse to sign the final decree, I went out and celebrated with some friends. I woke up very late the next morning. I was two hours away from where I had to be in one hour to sign the divorce papers.

I jumped out of bed, put on my flip flops and grabbed my bra. As I arrived in Shelton, I put my bra on in the car at a stop light. I arrived in court with unbrushed hair and in my pajamas an hour late. I was a mess, but thought I still looked better than the person on the other side of the courtroom – a six foot two inch man in a woman's dress. The only part of the decree I cared about was the clear finding of Amber's fraud, not dischargeable by bankruptcy.

Seeing Amber, I realized that each time I saw her, her ass was getting bigger and bigger. I said to myself, 'You wanted female hormones and you got them – and you got what you deserve – a big ass.'

I Go To London

On October 15, 2008, my divorce from Amber was final. Ten days later, I took a job as a massage therapist on a cruise ship. New cruise staff had to take a training course at the Steiner Academy in London. After arriving in London, I discovered that they had changed the term of my contract from six months to eight months and I was expected to sell $7,000 worth of their products a week to my clients. I decided to return home.

On the way back, I was stopped by the border patrol at JFK airport. They searched my bag four times while they detained me in a guarded room.

They sent me and my bag to another inspector. I asked why they were searching my bag so many times. He said it was because the computer showed an assault charge on my record.

I said, "Huh?" Then he asked me if I knew someone named Amber. "Oh," I said, "That's a person I used to be married to." He looked confused, but finally cleared me through to the next inspector.

When the new inspector opened my bag and saw my stuff jumbled up from all the searches, she looked surprised. "That bag is exactly like my life," I said. She asked what I meant. I said, "My life is a total mess." She passed me through and I was free to go.

Amber Appeals The Divorce

While I was in London, 32 days after signing the final divorce decree, Amber filed an appeal of the divorce. The deadline to file an appeal is 30 days, but somehow she was allowed to do it at 32 days.

A year later, in January, 2010, three judges of the Washington appellate court upheld the finding of fraud and the judgment ordering Amber to repay me the money she stole. I have not received any of the money, or had my personal property returned, as of yet. But I will continue to pursue Amber's compliance with the order, no matter how long it takes.

Back to Washington

While in London I kept thinking about my youngest daughter Jenifer, who was about ready to have her first baby, while her husband served in Iraq. When I got back, I went to St. George and stayed with her until her husband came home. My adorable grandson, Sebastian, was born on January 3, 2009.

My kids asked me to move back to St. George, but I felt that in case my legal trouble wasn't over yet, I didn't want to take a chance on their families getting involved in the drama.

I loved Washington and decided to move to the Seattle area. I stayed with a friend in Bellevue, until I got my massage business going.

In December, 2009, after three years of waking up every day saying, *This is not my life,* I woke up and realized that this *is* my life. It's mine and I need to accept it. Many people go through much worse ordeals in their lives.

Since I was 15 years old, I had focused all my attention on taking care of my family. Now that it was just me, I felt lost and without a purpose. I had been through so much confusion and upset the last few years, I felt I needed to take a break from my life and my surroundings and take a fresh look at everything.

I Go To Thailand

Someone I had met through Events and Adventures told me that there was a great massage school in Chaing Mai, Thailand. The idea intrigued me. And it was perfect timing for me to get a change of scenery. I figured out that I could go for two months and take as many classes as I could during that time. In January, 2010, I bought my plane ticket and left within two weeks. That was the beginning of my new life.

When I got to Thailand I realized I had never experienced true relaxation before. I felt amazingly free. On the second day, I decided to do a Zip Line (extreme repelling), and had a really cool experience. I felt like, 'Oh My God – I'm completely free. I can make all my own choices.'

If it hadn't been for the drama and trauma I'd been through in my life, I would not be able to appreciate my freedom the way I do now. If I hadn't married Chuck, I would have married some other man right away anyway – another abusive person.

My next adventure was visiting Tiger Kingdom and spending one-on-one time with some tigers. I was surprised that I wasn't afraid to touch them. I felt their powerful energy and amazing strength. I suddenly realized that I was strong and powerful, too. It made a huge impact on how I saw myself.

From that moment, I promised myself, I would move on with my life and leave the past behind. I was my own person now and wanted to focus on who I was, what I wanted and what I needed. I knew that I was important, that I mattered.

I called my daughter Jenifer and asked her how she thought I had changed over the last three years. She said, "You used to try to fix everyone else problems and not worry about your own. Now you're more focused on your own needs. You're more positive and have better self-esteem than ever."

I asked my daughter Jamie the same question. Her answer was, "Now when I try to tell you my problems, after a couple of minutes you say, 'I have to go.' You used to listen to my problems for hours."

This IS My Life

Now I wanted to be in my life. I was very excited to come back from Thailand and resume my new life that included my massage business. I had no desire to leave or change my situation. I felt completely at peace.

My daughter Rachel was expecting her first child in March. I wanted to get back before little Hailey was born. I didn't make it. I got to St. George 10 hours after she arrived.

I felt really different when I got back to Washington. I was so much more positive and hopeful about the future. My self-esteem skyrocketed. I wanted to move forward and build a foundation for my new life. This time things would be very different.

Since then, my business has been going very well. I believe that the extreme physical pain I suffered during the Amber episode made me a much better massage therapist. Many of my clients experience immediate and long-lasting relief from chronic pain. I feel so fortunate to be able to help people get rid of their pain. Massage therapy is definitely part of my new purpose in life.

In 2010, I decided to get rid of my trailer. It was never a home to me. I sold it and bought a nice condo near Seattle. I purchased my new home by myself. Every day I am so grateful for the freedom I have to make my own decisions, no matter how small: what colors to paint my walls, what furnishings I want. Since I had lost all of my property, I could start from scratch choosing things of my own taste.

I love the way my life is turning out – a life that has made it possible for me to appreciate everything, including who I am as a person. I have no regrets about any part of my life. No matter what challenges I face in the future, I know I will always be all right. I am a complete, whole person. I wish everyone could experience what I feel – I am 100% O.K. with every part of my life.

Made in the USA
Charleston, SC
15 November 2010